Simple Strands

A simple strand of ribbon, silk, leather or cord elegantly highlights a Silver focal pendant or bead.

Ribbons and cords are finished by knotting the cords inside caps or crimping special ends that have loops already attached to the crimp.

Finishing a Necklace

String all the decorative beads as desired.

1. Add a crimp bead and slip the wire through one end of a closed jump ring. A crimp bead is a little tube bead that the beading wire slides through at the end of a strand.

2. Loop the beading wire back though the crimp bead to double up with the strung wire and create a loop to hold the closure.

3. Squeeze the crimp bead to hold the wire loop secure. Crimping pliers separate the beading wire in a special indent in the jaws as they clamp down on the crimp bead.

After the crimp is firmly squeezed, position the crimp in the round indent of the pliers to squeeze both channels together.

4. Slide a clam shell shaped crimp cover over the crimp tube and press the sides together to make a ball-shaped bead hiding the crimp.

5. Slip the end of the wire back through several beads to hide the end. Cut off excess wire.

6. Attach jump rings to any necklace properly. Open and close jump rings by bending the rings **side** to **side** until they meet exactly.

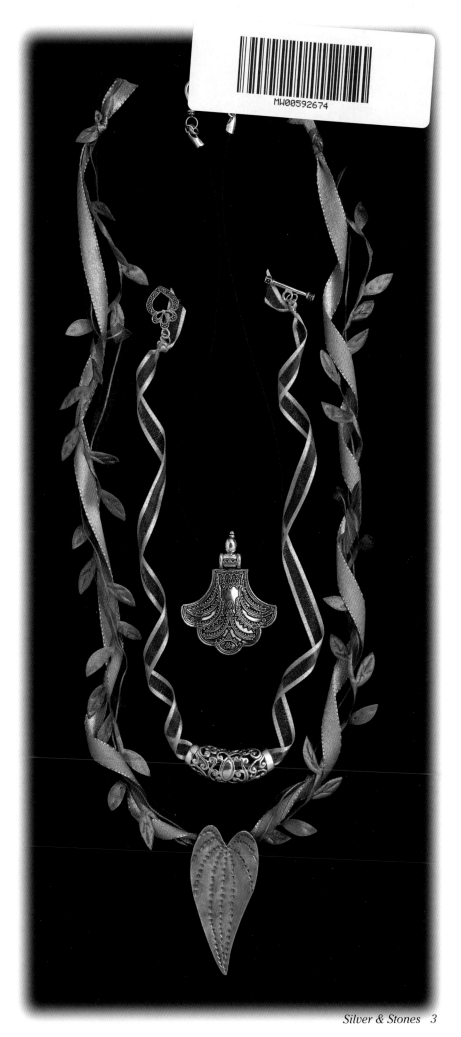

Basic Supplies

Components used to make jewelry are called findings. These include crimps, crimp covers, jump rings and clasps.

Purchase the best tools possible, as the ease and quality of your work will increase with the quality of the tools.

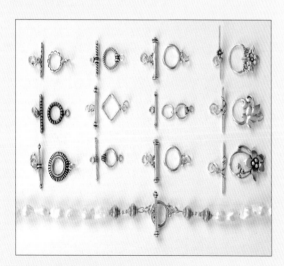

Toggle Clasps are a ring (or alternate shape) and an inserted bar that intersects enabling the strand to open and close easily, yet guarantee a secure hold when closed. The toggle should match the style of the necklace.

Simple Basics

Beading Wire

The best known string for simple strands is called beading wire. Soft Flex and Beadalon are popular brands. Beading wire is made of stainless steel cables wrapped with a flexible nylon coating that makes the entire strand soft, bendable, and strong.

The spool label describes the number of strands, the diameter, the length, and sometimes the breaking tolerance, for example 15 lbs.

Always use the strongest wire possible that will fit through the holes in your beads. I prefer wire with a diameter between .012" - .020".

Tools

You need flush cutters for beading wire and 2 pair of needle-nose pliers to open and close jump rings, and hold small parts.

Round-nose pliers are used to turn wire into loops.

A needle tool or awl is helpful to slide a crimp bead to its right place.

Crimping pliers are indispensable because they have special grooves in the jaws for crimping.

Another useful item is a bead board, a large flat board with curving rows, marked with measurements and made to keep beads from rolling. This tool is an indispensable nest for holding beads while you decide what goes where and in what order. It also shows how long the necklace will be.

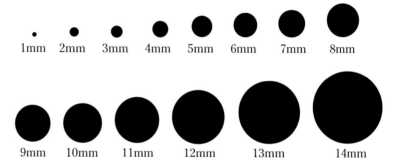

Bead sizes are measured in millimeters.

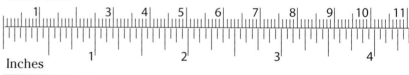

Care and Cleaning of Silver

Sterling tarnishes when exposed to air. You can slow this process by storing pieces, including unfinished pieces and wire, in a plastic bag or air-tight container.

Clean tarnished Silver with a chemically treated cloth called sunshine cloth, or with liquid or paste Silver cleaner and a cloth.

If using a liquid chemical dip, check the tolerance of pearls or stones before immersing a piece in a chemical bath.

Glass bead shown by Rick Shelby

Beads come in assorted sizes, colors, shapes and finishes. They are available in beautiful glass, stone, silver and other materials.

The face of a bead looks different from the end. Look at the side of a bead to visualize how it will appear in your necklace.

Examples of textured beads that are stamped and formed

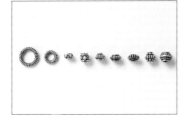

Spacer beads define the rhythm of a piece and separate the stones. Having just the right spacer makes all the difference.

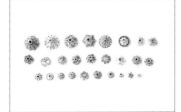

Bead caps fit over the hole of a stone or bead and provide a decorative finish that complements the entire bead. Caps also hide multiple strands.

Examples of high quality silver beads

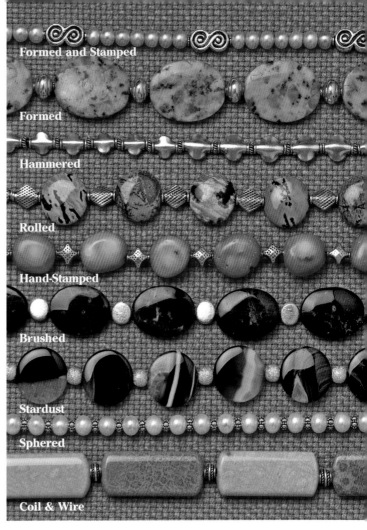

Formed and Stamped

Formed

Hammered

Rolled

Hand-Stamped

Brushed

Stardust

Sphered

Coil & Wire

Finishes on Silver

Silver beads differ in quality. Look to see if your bead is hand-formed with soldered components, hand-rolled, or machine pressed. Train your eye to differentiate the quality.

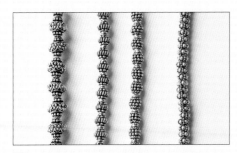

Silver is sold in strands by weight at bead markets. Keep in mind how heavy your finished piece may become.

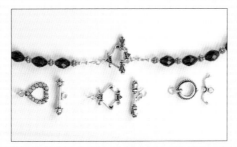

Choose a toggle to match the style of piece you are making. Test the closure for ease of opening and closing.

You can use hook style clasps or magnets to connect strands. Be sure to match the style of the necklace.

Pearls - The value of a pearl depends on size, quality, color and finish (pages 8 - 9).

Silver beads - Store silver in zipper bags or a sealed container (pages 6 - 7).

Stones - Earth stones are usually created and colored by nature or dyed in various processes (pages 28 - 31).

Silver & Stones 5

Simply Silver

The elegant Silver beads now referred to as Bali beads coined their name from their origin, in Bali, Indonesia; however, a similar style of bead is also made in Thailand, India and China.

The history of these beads reaches back to the 16th century when Hindu craftsman from Java sought refuge in Bali from imposed Islamic rule. Today traditions of each culture are reflected in the decorative styles of the beads. For example, modern Javanese silversmiths excel in fine filigree work and 'plin', a style of shiny flat surfaces and clean, streamlined joints.

Balinese smiths are skilled in granulation, in which minute spheres of Silver and rings of wire are intricately arranged and soldered into beautiful geometric patterns. Although the original Balinese Silver bead designs were derived from traditional gold jewelry, modern designs reflect diverse multicultural motifs that change as smiths become exposed to international trends and demands.

A popular style depicting floral, leaf, nautical and dragonflies or butterflies emerged from the Karen Hilltribe in northern Bali. The prosperity of the regions often relies on the demand of each tribe's styles and craftsmanship.

Necklaces (page 6)

Necklace 1: 33mm Thai Hilltribe Silver flower pendant • Sterling mesh chain • Basic supplies

Necklace 2: Tooled Bali Silver beads (13mm, 17,mm, 23mm) • 6mm Silver spacer beads • Sterling Cable • Basic supplies

Necklace 3: Tooled Silver beads (12mm, 18mm, 33mm) • 9 x 20mm Silver Cone beads • Hammered Silver beads (10mm, 20mm) • Basic supplies

Necklace 4: 40mm Hill tribe Silver Flower • Hilltribe silver leaves (26 x 45mm, 18 x 30mm, 10 x 22mm) • 3mm Silver spacer beads • 34mm Silver 'Noodle' tube beads • Basic supplies

Lariat Necklace (page 7): 3mm Silver chain • 7mm Silver jump rings • 8 - 17mm Silver charms • 24mm Silver marcasite toggle clasp • Basic supplies

Lariat Clasps

Lariats: Lariats are usually long necklaces with the connecting clasp in the front.

Large toggles are perfect for creating lariats. Add charms from the loop to create the dangling focal points.

In this case the toggle acts as a focus as well as the clasp. Charms are attached with jump rings and add weight or tension to the toggle, which is needed to keep it closed.

Marcasite clasp: The style of silver shown in this toggle is called marcasite.

Marcasite silver is faceted to reflect the light, creating an illusion of set stone.

Pearls are the gemstones of the sea. They form in the shells of abalone, oysters and mussels (mollusks).

The difference between a natural pearl and a cultured pearl is that natural pearls form as a chance occurrence in nature, while cultured pearls are the result of manipulated intervention with nature. In cultured pearls, one or more nuclei (foreign object, usually a bit of shell) are implanted into a living mollusk. This stimulates production of nacre, the silky and lustrous mother of pearl substance, which builds up layer by layer, eventually creating a pearl.

Imitation pearls are made of glass, plastic, or shell beads dipped in ground fish scales and lacquered with pearlescence. Cultured pearls possess an inner glow, while imitation pearls reflect a surface shine. A genuine cultured pearl will have a gritty feel when run over the edge of your teeth, but the fake pearl will not.

Pearl quality is judged by luster, size, shape, surface, color and weight. There are two grading systems, the AAA system, AAA being highest quality and A-D, D being lowest quality.

Stringing of pearls is a consideration regarding the value of pearl jewelry. Pearl 'make' is the scrutinizing attention in which pearls are matched for pearl size, shape, color, luster and complexion.

Cultured Saltwater Pearls are farmed in saltwater, with a single pearl grown in each oyster. Most abundantly farmed in Indonesia, Burma, Thailand, the Philippines, Australia and Tahiti.

Abalone Pearls need 8-10 years to develop and result in a variety of shapes. The colors resemble an 'oil slick' of royal blues and greens, magentas, purples, and soft metallics.

Akoya Pearls are prized for their exact round shapes. They grow in cooler ocean water temperatures and require anywhere from 6-24 months to cultivate. Akoya pearls possess an exceptional luster and color and display a variety of colors, such as blue, green, pink, rose, cream, white, silver and gold.

Cultured Freshwater Pearls are cultivated in fresh water in Japan and China. A single mussel may produce twenty pearls or more within one year, because the mussel can produce several pearls at once. This makes freshwater pearls more affordable. Generally freshwater pearls are smaller, with irregular shapes. Several pieces of tissue are grafted into the mussel, producing odd pearls with a crinkly surface often referred to as rice pearls. These tiny pearls reflect a glassy luster and are relatively durable. Recently the Chinese have succeeded in creating higher quality freshwater pearls, very similar to ocean pearls, making an attractive strand of pearls more affordable and available.

South Sea Pearls are exquisite in quality and beauty showcasing a silvery white color. Large oysters produce large lustrous pearls. South Sea pearls are exclusively grown in tropical and semi-tropical locations, usually off the coasts of Australia, Indonesia, and the Philippines.

Tahitian Pearls, also referred to as black South Sea pearls, are grown in a large oyster with a black lip. These large oysters produce pearls known for their dark colors and large size. Each pearl requires approximately six years to develop. The water must be pure and the temperature dictates the luster of the pearl, making the development of each pearl dependent on its environment.

Mabe Pearls are grown adjacent to the inside shell of the Mabe oyster. They are flat on one side and display exquisite colors, ranging from light pinks, to bluish shades. Mabe pearls, while attached to the oyster,are blister pearls. The blister is then cut and filled in with a resin and covered with a mother of pearl. Mabe pearls are cultured in saltwater oysters in Japan, Indonesia, Australia and French Polynesia.

Blister Pearls are freshwater pearls, grown against the inside shell, and are often cut to include a portion of the host shell. They make unique focal specimens for use as pendants, wrapping wire and beading.

Keshi Pearls are distinct because the oyster has actually cast out the nucleus. They are made entirely of nacre and possess a bright luster. Their variable shapes are appealing to jewelers who incorporate them into unique and innovative designs.

Pearls are Perfect

Pearls are timeless, classic, elegant and abundant. They vary greatly in quality and price, and seeing row after row of pearls can be overwhelming. Pearl shapes include round, button, pear, potato, baroque (irregular), coin and ringed. Blister pearls are manipulated to grow in special shapes or colors and include portions of the host shell.

Pearls can be dyed to offer an exquisite range of designer colors. There are also synthetic pearls that range from plastic to glass. Swarovski now produces crystal pearls with a special simulated pearl coating. Traders also sell 'shell' pearls, which are ground shells with a simulated pearl coating.

Pearls are measured in millimeters and are drilled with very small holes, so be sure to take this into account when choosing beading wire.

Necklace 1: 8mm Pearls • 3mm Silver spacer beads • Basic supplies
Necklace 2: Pearls (4mm, 6mm) • 3mm Silver spacer beads • 4mm Swarovski beads • Basic supplies
Necklace 3: 6mm Pearls • 10mm Silver hollow filigree beads • Basic supplies
Necklace 4: 6mm Pearls • 5mm Silver spacer beads • 18 - 22mm Pink Peruvian Opal stones • Basic supplies

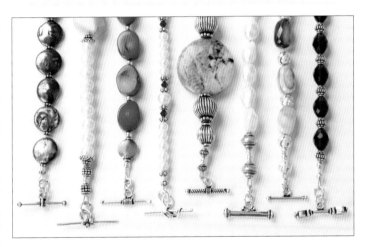

Comfortable Clasps & Lengths

The standard lengths for necklaces are 16", 18" and 24" and 36"; however, the lengths will fall differently on each person.

There are special clasps that allow an exceptionally long strand to be doubled.

Be sure to test your lengths visually as well as measure before designing your jewelry.

The consistent sizing of pearls allows beautiful rhythms in design. You can also add highlights of color to your pieces with glass, crystal and gemstones.

Tiny spacers also define the rhythm and highlight the accents. Be sure to do the math.

Calculate not only the number of accents you will need, but the length of the sequences.

Unique Treasures... Pearls & Silver

Combine the luxurious luster of pearls with the shimmer of silver for a stunning set of necklaces you will treasure for both evening and day wear.

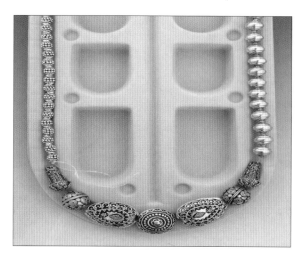

Using a Bead Board

Special boards may be purchased for designing necklaces and jewelry. They have a soft surface that helps keep beads from rolling. Use a bead board to quickly arrange variations while determining appropriate sequences.

Usually there are recessed spaces to keep an assortment of beads handy while you are designing.

Often there are multiple rows for necklace designs. These rows make it easy to position beads upright to see what they may look like when finished.

Each necklace design pictured reflects individual tastes. Combine your beads in several arrangements to see which one works best. Consider all options before committing to the perfect design.

The arrangement of beads should flow with rhythm and balance.

Necklace 1: 10mm Semi-Baroque (irregular) Pearls
• 19 - 33mm shaped Silver beads • Basic supplies

Necklace 2: 12mm Coin Pearls • Silver spacer beads (1mm, 5mm) • 50mm Silver flower pendant • Basic supplies

Necklace 3: 5mm Pearls • 13mm Formed Silver beads
• 52mm Silver flower pendant • Basic supplies

Necklace 4: 10mm Pearls • 1 - 3mm Silver spacer beads
• Assorted Thai Silver flowers • Basic supplies

Silver Shimmers

Graduated stones are exceptionally attractive because they use rhythm to establish the focus. Disk-shaped stones carry a heavy visual weight and work well in graduated design.

Cutting and polishing stones is a skill and is indicated by the price of the stone. Polish should reflect a high luster. Shapes and thicknesses are delicate, and sometimes smaller or thinner stones can be more difficult to fashion than larger ones.

Consider wearing the necklace and the effect of smooth or sharp edges on the skin.

Necklaces (page 12)

Necklace 1: 13mm Pearl Coin beads • 1mm Silver spacer beads • 10 - 15mm Thai Silver beads • Basic supplies

Necklace 2: 12mm Purple faceted glass beads • 5mm Silver spacer beads • 30mm Bali Silver bead • 25mm Bali Silver beads • Basic supplies

Necklace 3: 8 - 15mm round Pink Rhodanite stones • 3 - 10mm Silver bead caps • 6mm Silver spacer beads • Basic supplies

Silver Links...
Just for Fun

Create a fantastic and charming necklace with a super-size link chain and a toggle. This neck-size version of the traditional charm bracelet allows you to mix and match odd collected beads, wonderful colors, and found objects.

You don't even need to finish all at once. Just add charms and dangles over time. Choose an appropriate number or size of jump rings to accommodate the movement of the dangles.

Links Necklace with Charms:
18mm Oval Silver links • 4mm Silver jump rings • Silver head pins • Assorted Glass, Silver and Pearl beads • Assorted Silver charms • Basic supplies

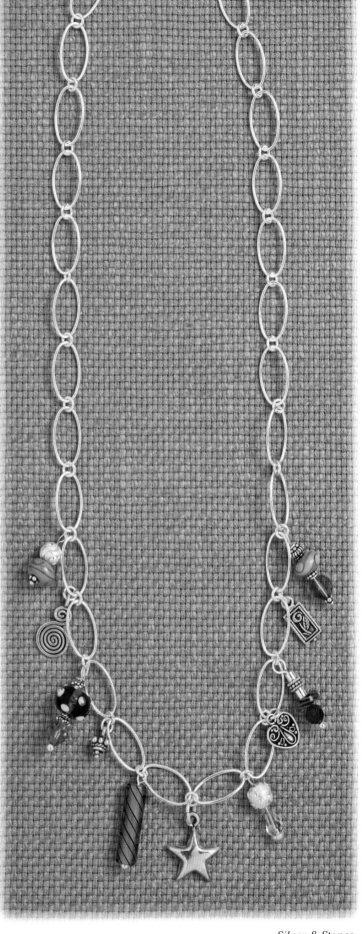

Exotic & Ethnic

Tribal customs, religious practices, skilled tradition, and availability of natural stones and resources all define styles of adornment within specific cultures.

Today we have the resources to mingle designs from various cultures, creating a striking mix of color and style.

Many beautiful ethnic focal beads and turquoise come from Tibet, Afghanistan, India, Thailand, Indonesia, Vietnam and Africa.

Choosing Components

First consider color. Generally, the stones from parts of the world are grouped together. For example, stones from Tibet usually complement each other.

However, not everything goes together. African millefiori glass beads may not look right with the Vietnamese pendant unless the designer skillfully used that combination as an element of contrast.

When designing a piece, there should be no question as to the focus of the piece and the supporting stones and silver should not compete with that focus.

Necklaces (page 14)

Necklace 1: 22 - 35mm Chrysocolla stones • 3mm Silver Spacer beads • 37mm Silver toggle clasp (the designer toggle clasp by Saki Silver is intended to be worn in the front of the necklace as a focal point in the design) • Basic supplies

Necklace 2: 40mm Polished Fossil rectangle stones • 5mm Silver spacer beads • 35mm Petroglyph Inscribed Noga Shell head bead from Tibet • Basic supplies

Necklace 3: 44mm Tribal Rhodanite pendant by the Taureg Tribe in North Africa • 38mm Noga Shell beads from Tibet • 20mm Silver beads (hand-rolled hollow beads from Thailand) • Basic supplies
Tip: This necklace also has a carved Rhodanite scarab in a bezel on a clasp. By Nina Designs.

Vietnamese Pendant

This beautiful turquoise donut is framed with sterling and displays a delicate silver figure Kwan Yin, the Asian goddess of mercy and compassion.

The necklace is strung with sterling and faceted jade, another stone popular in the region. The silver is a stamped floral pattern which complements the feminine nature of the deity. Both the color and the origin of the stones are grouped in harmony.

Necklace (page 15)
58 x 75mm Turquoise pendant • 3mm Jade beads • 9mm Silver beads • Basic supplies

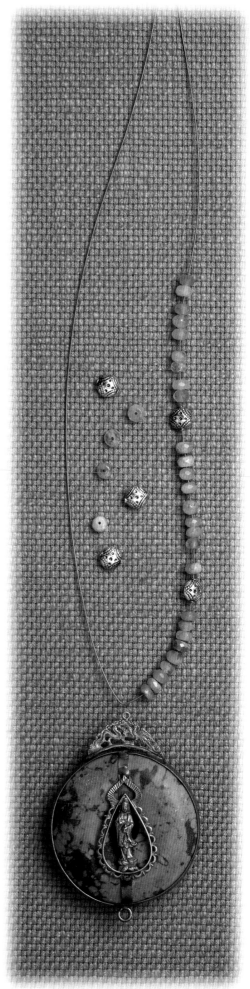

Turquoise & Coral

Use of turquoise in adornment dates back as early as 6000 BC when the Egyptians skillfully fashioned the stones into amulets and charms. Other cultures that embraced the bright blue stone were the Aztecs and Southwest Native Americans.

The quality of the stone varies greatly with color and size. Finer turquoise is sold by the gram. The color reveals where the turquoise was mined with bright blue veins originating in Egypt and the Southern and Southwestern United States while greener varieties are pre-dominant throughout Asia and Australia.

Turquoise has also been dyed to enhance the color or to give the stone an altogether different color, such as yellow turquoise. Dyed turquoise begins as a white stone and is dyed with an electro-plating process to assure the fastness of the color.

Price will generally dictate whether the stones are real or dyed. Polish, cut and purity also determine the value. Turquoise found with veins of man-ganese often bears the nickname spider turquoise. It is often sold in nuggets, its natural state.

Pearl Bracelets

A quick way to make a bracelet is by using memory wire.

Finish the ends by gluing the last pearl or by creating a hook and dangling additional pearls (see the center bracelet above).

Add Crystal beads or special crystal spacers to highlight pearls in an attractive way (see the outside bracelet above).

Necklaces (page 16)

Necklace 1: 30 x 42mm Repoussee Chank Shell beads (Tibetan inscribed) • 17mm Natural Coral chunks • 100mm Thai Silver tube beads • 4mm silver spacer beads • Basic supplies
Note: The tubes unscrew at each end so you can string the beads; however, the beads must be strung in the direction of the removable end; in other words, from the center bead outwards.

Necklace 2: 42mm Sterling Silver Dragonfly bead by AD Adornments • 10mm Polished Turquoise Briolettes (from China) • Basic supplies

Necklace 3: 35mm Sand Dollar bead (Thai Hill Tribe silver) • 22mm Hollow Shell beads • Chank Shell spacer beads (3mm, 8mm) • 24 - 43mm Red Coral Spikes • 10mm Barrel Coral beads (showing natural coral veins) • 22mm Peruvian Opal pol-ished stones • 4mm Silver spacer beads • Basic supplies • Clasp by Jess Imports

Necklace 4: 23mm Chinese Turquoise Stones • 30mm Bezeled Chank Shell Center stone • 20 - 27mm Capped Coral and Shell beads (from Tibet) • 53mm Rolled Brass Bicone Beads (from India) • 5mm Silver spacer beads • Noga Shell spacer beads (3mm, 8mm) • Basic supplies

Bracelets (page 17)

Center Bracelet:
7mm double Pearls • Memory Wire • 5mm Silver spacer beads • mm Decorative head pins • 5mm jump rings
TIPS: Use pliers to form each end of the Memory Wire into a closed loop. Slip a pearl and spacer bead onto a head pin. Form the end into a closed loop. Attach a dan-gle to each end of the bracelet with jump rings.

Outside Bracelet:
7mm Pearls • 3mm Swarovski Crystal spacers • 2mm Silver spacer beads • Basic supplies

Necklace 1: Etched Lampwork glass beads by JoAnn Zekowski (10mm, 14mm, 20mm)
• Silver Bali beads (6mm, 10mm) • 4mm Jasper Garnet mini beads • 4mm Agate mini round beads • Basic supplies

Necklace 2: 4mm Onyx Faceted Beads • 3mm Tourmaline Crystals • 5mm 3-hole Marcasite Sterling spacer bars • 2mm Silver spacer beads • 35mm 3-hole Marcasite end clasp • Basic supplies

Necklace (page 19): 43mm Matte Lampwork Moon Bead with Asian Characters "Peace" by Tracy Nelligan of Turtle Moon Arts • 7mm Bali Silver beads • 4 mm Coral Heishi Beads • 17mm Silver Cones • Basic supplies

Multiple Strands

Repetition strengthens a design theme. Particularly in the case of small strands, repetition adds visual weight and value. Multiple strands also give the impression of abundance and luxury. Shape and size is important since the technical aspects of stringing can be a challenge.

For example, all the strands must pass through each focal bead, occasionally making this a tight fit. Take into account the size of the holes when stringing beads. Also develop an appreciation for small bead strands and their effective use in design. Remember that smaller beads require a smaller stringing wire, and a smaller diameter crimp. Do the math when aligning sequences - one stone off will create a bulging strand.

Each strand should be equal or graduated in length to allow the necklace to lie properly. Make sure you test the curvature of the neck when planning a design with parallel stands. A draped sequence will demand more planning and testing.

Special Finishing

In several of the necklaces shown, the strands attach to a single jump ring that hides the crimped strands inside the cone or cap at the end of the necklace. This jump ring can be inside or outside the cone, depending on what can be reached when working the crimps.

I prefer connecting to a soldered jump ring and then connecting the ring with wire, making a loop or eye connected inside, then inserted through the cone and again looped outside the tip of the cone.

It's good to have several size cones on hand because it's hard to visualize the fit without actually testing it.

Designer Findings

Several clasps are designed with multiple strands in mind. The marcasite silver clasp shown has individual holes to accommodate each strand. In this case the strands were stayed by additional beads and then crimped on the outside of the clasp.

It is also possible to knot the cords and hide them on the inside of the clasp, using the knot as a stop. A chandelier style finding is also appropriate for finishing multiple strands depending on the number of rings or holes.

An additional clasp is attached to the chandelier to finish the work.

Spacers

Multiple spacers look like little bars with several holes. The spacer is viewed sideways and helps to separate the strands, preventing them from tangling.

These spacers can also be designed as special motifs as in the case of the matching marcasite Silver spacers and clasp shown.

Necklace 1: 20mm Red Lampwork bead • 15mm Coral nuggets • 6mm Black Onyx beads • 10mm Silver disc beads • 2mm Silver spacer beads • Basic supplies

Necklace 2: 30mm Pink and Cobalt Blue Lampwork bead • 15mm Pink Coral (dyed) cross-cut ovals • 15mm Silver beads • 10mm Silver spacer beads • Basic supplies

Necklace 3: 30mm Green Lampwork bead • 20mm Russian Serpentine beads • 45mm African Brass beads • 5mm Silver spacer beads • Basic supplies

All blown glass lampwork beads are by Rodney Andrews

Focal Beads

Choosing a focal bead is a personal decision. Beads are often souvenirs of a place or time, perhaps a piece made by someone dear, a gift, or just an irresistible work of art, as in blown glass beads.

Pendants are particularly appropriate for focal points. Consider how the pendant will dangle from the necklace. Think about the visual weight of the piece in relation to the rest of the necklace. A heavy piece would be out of balance with delicate beads.

Shape – Often a triangle shape pointing downward looks best. Take into account whether the bead will bulge out from the rest of the necklace creating an awkward balance.

Hole Size – Many blown glass beads have larger holes that work well with cords and ribbons, but will dangle on thin wires.

Colors and Textures – Be inspired by beautiful colors and interesting textures. Surface design comes into play with many focal pieces as a smooth glass piece may not be suitably paired with rough nuggets.

Place a small bead on either side of a large focal bead to soften the transition between beads. This also keeps beads from rubbing and scratching against each other, preventing cracks and breakage.

Focal Stones (above)
Ethiopian cross • Cast Brass African pendant • Chinese Carved jade oval barrel • Chinese Carved Cinnabar round bead • Chinese Carved Serpentine pendant • Raku Ceramic Butterfly

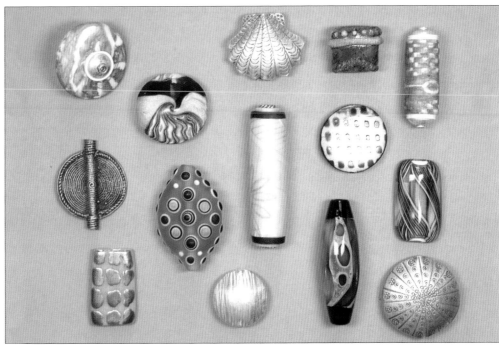

Assorted collection of ceramic, lampwork glass, polymer, brass and silver beads

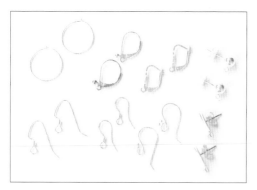

Earring findings are available in several shapes and sizes... hoops, dangle clips, fish hook shapes and posts.

Choose the style that you find the most comfortable to wear, and the easiest to hang from your ears.

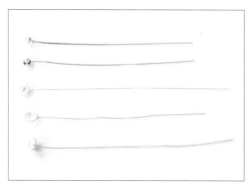

Head pins and Eye pins are designed to insert a sequence of stones onto a finding.

Trim pin to size. Bend the wire to one side. Using round-nose pliers, grasp the end and turn a loop into a ring.

Open and close the ring from side to side to attach the dangle.

Chandelier findings are Silver or gold filigree with several tiny holes or loops for connecting additional pieces.

They can be used as earrings or as end findings on necklaces with multiple strands.

Coordinate the dangling parts to balance with the size of the earring, and the space between the holes.

Earring findings vary in their small details and you will find a personal preference once you begin designing.

My favorite is a very simple wire and loop with a ball. This enables an earring to slip over the ear wire and attach without jump rings.

Adding jump rings will lengthen the earring and allow it more movement. Pay attention to the direction of the intersecting loops, making sure the earring will hang to the front.

Lever-back earrings have a mechanism that closes back after it is inserted into the ear.

Post earrings come in many styles and have little loops attached for dangling parts.

Hoop earrings are a great finding, but be sure your bead has a hole big enough to slide through the hoop.

Sequences of the stones, pearls or gems should be balanced and simple and will define the length of the finished earring. A simple charm is also effective as an earring.

Make a Dangle Earring

1. String beads on a head pin in the desired order.

2. Cut the post of the pin with wire cutters, ½ inch from the top of the bead.

3. Bend the post to a 90° angle with round-nose pliers.

4. With round nose pliers, bend the post to form a loop.

5. Curl the loop until it touches the post and forms a smooth secure circle.

6. Attach an earring wire to the loop.

Elegance for Earrings

Matching earrings complete a jewelry ensemble. The goal is to coordinate the pieces by repeating some elements in the necklace.

A simple way to make earrings is to use a head pin. Head pins are long wires with a decorative heads soldered to one end. The diameter of the wire will vary and the style of the head will range from a flat disk to various sizes and shapes of decoration, often involving tiny balls. Be sure to check the diameter of the hole of the pearl or stone with the head pin.

Insert the pin though a sequence of beads and the remaining wire is bent into a round loop. The loop is then attached to the ear wire.

If you don't have pierced ears, you can find special lever clamp earrings with loops for attaching dangling parts.

Earring dangles can also be connected by wrapping the head pin wire around itself after the loop is made.

In this process the loop extends slightly upward from the last bead. After the loop is turned the wire is wrapped around the extended length.

Earring 1: 18mm Lapis oval stones • 2mm head pins • Ear posts

Earring 2: 8mm Turquoise Briolette stones • 3mm Silver spacer beads • 18mm earring hoops

Earring 3: 16mm Thai Silver beads • 8mm Black glass beads • 2mm Silver spacer bead • 2mm head pins • 20mm earring hoops

Earring 4: 10 x 23mm Thai Hill Tribe Silver leaves • Silver earring wires

Earring 5: 12mm Formed Silver beads • 5mm Amber Swarovski crystals • Head pins • Ear posts

Earring 6: 12 x 31mm Silver Chandelier dangles • Silver earring wires

Earring 7: 4mm Turquoise Swarovski beads • 3mm Decorative head pins • 25 x 37mm Silver Chandelier dangles • Silver earring wires

Earring 8: 7mm Pearl beads • 3mm Decorative head pins • 22 x 25mm Silver Chandelier dangles • Silver earring wires

Briolettes

Today's market has become a designer's paradise.

Traditions still invoke the days of kings and queens, and shimmering gems or pearls can make a royal collection for any beauty. Today's popular trends include little droplets, or teardrop faceted gems, crystals and stones called 'Briolettes'.

These have a hole drilled from side to side across the top of the bead, allowing the bead to dangle and set apart from the main strand.

Individually Briolettes stand out as highlights, but grouped together they create the illusion of several strands together.

As trends develop, new cuts are fashioned that become popular. Technology has allowed stones to be fashioned in many shapes and forms to the designer's advantage.

Larger stones that do not require cabochon settings are now available and modern materials such as polymer clay enable designers to fashion unique focal beads.

Vintage Accents

Using antique parts in design acknowledges the timeless value of style and respect for fashionable trends. This helps to add contrast to otherwise mundane work.

At different times, styles of beads will become popular and fade, only to resurface as new-found treasures.

The term 'vintage' denotes popularity from a specific time.

Examples of this are vintage Czechoslovakian glass beads, vintage resin beads, vintage bakelite beads and African Trade beads.

Using beads that are less costly but prized for heritage adds unique value to a piece.

Necklaces (page 24)

Necklace 1:
30mm Camouflage Jasper lentil shaped beads • 5mm Smoky Pearl pear beads • 2mm Silver spacer beads • Basic supplies

Necklace 2:
18 x 25mm Blue Goldstone Briolettes • 5mm Pearl pear beads • 2mm Silver spacer beads • Basic supplies

Necklaces (page 25)

Necklace 1:
30 x 30mm Polymer Clay transferred Icon bead • 20mm African Brass Coil triangle beads • 25mm Purple agate polished stones • Brass spacer beads (3mm, 11mm) • Basic supplies

Necklace 2:
25 x 62mm Polymer Clay Mokume Gane bead • 20mm African Brass Cast beads • 8mm Potato pearls • 2mm Brass spacer beads • 8mm Noga shell spacer beads • Basic supplies

Leave a Small Space on the Ends

Leave a space to allow some flexibility on the end between the clasp and crimp bead and where the first bead starts. This will allow play in the necklace end so it will drape nicely around the neck.

The loose end should be clipped and tucked into the next bead.

Placing a small bead after the ring and before the crimp helps to ease pressure on the crimp.

Some necklaces are double crimped for added security.

There is no limit to the shape and cut of rocks, minerals and gems. Today's shapes are large and bold, faceted and polished. When choosing a shape, be aware of how it will bend when placed next to another stone.

Square or rectangle stones will need a round or pebble bead or sequence of beads between the stones in order to curve around the neck and flex properly. Be sure to allow enough give when you are finishing your work to allow the necklace to turn.

Also keep in mind the mood of the work. Brushed or laser cut silver will give a modern flare, while filigree and ethnic styles will denote a more traditional or earthy design. Sparkles and shimmers are appropriate anytime.

Put Spacer Beads Between Larger Beads

Spacer beads are usually small; either Silver or glass seed beads will work.

Notice in the photos below how the small spacer beads allow the necklace to bend and drape without 'holes' between the beads.

Necklace 1: 13mm Faceted Sardonyx oval stone beads • 7mm Silver laser cut spacer beads • Basic supplies

Necklace 2: 20mm Polished disk Sardonyx stone beads • 5mm Silver Stardust spacer beads • Basic supplies

Necklace 3: 25mm Polished disk Blue Sodalite oval stone beads • 8mm flat Silver spacer beads • 5mm Silver spacer beads • Basic supplies

Necklace 4: 30mm Kiwi Quartz Polished oval stone beads • Silver spacer beads (5mm, 8mm) • Basic supplies

Necklace 5: 30mm Pink Zebra stone beads • 13mm Silver round corrugated beads • 5 mm Silver spacer beads • Basic supplies

Beads without spacer beads

Tip: Use a spacer bar inside of the larger bead when it has an extra large hole. This will keep small spacer beads from slipping inside of the large bead and will cover the wire in an attractive way.

Beads with spacer beads

The necklace drapes in a smooth and pleasing curve when spacers are used between the beads

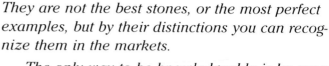

Rock & Stone Identification

Your personal gem collection is a reflection of tastes and insight to your creativity. The cut, color and size of the stone usually relates to an idea you have in mind of how it is going to be used – or the amount you have budgeted.

Keep in mind the artistry is in the design of the jewelry, not how expensive the stone is.

The following table reflects popular stones, shown in a variety of cuts intended for design.

They are not the best stones, or the most perfect examples, but by their distinctions you can recognize them in the markets.

The only way to be knowledgeable is by experience. It takes time to be able to recognize not only the specimen, but also a nice polish, a pure color, a favorite cut, and a good price.

Every time you design a piece, you will learn more information about stones.

Druzy Quartz

Quartz

Quartz is the most common mineral on the face of the Earth. It is formed as crystals and is contained in nearly every rock type. Its name originates from the ancient Greek word krustallos, meaning clear ice. Varieties of quartz are identified by color and quality.

Milky Quartz – cloudy white

Rock Crystal – clear

Rose Quartz – January Birthstone
Rose Quartz is pink to reddish pink.

Smoky Quartz

Smoky Quartz is brown to smoky gray.

Druzy Quartz

Druzy Quartz has tiny quartz crystals covering the surface of the stone. It can be vividly colored with natural metallic deposits of titanium coated in a special process.

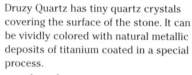

Rose Quartz

Amethyst – February Birthstone

Amethyst is recognized for its distinctively lavender purple color, ranging from crystal to milky quartz. The name "amethyst" comes from a Greek word meaning "not drunken." It was believed amethyst would protect its owner from intoxication.

Australia, Brazil, Madagascar, Canada, Germany India, Sri Lanka, USA, Uruguay

Amethyst & Citrine

Citrine – November Birthstone

Citrine is any quartz crystal or cluster that is yellow to orange, a color that is rare in nature but is often created by heating Amethyst.

Ametrine

Ametrine is a popular gemstone that is a mixture of half amethyst and half citrine.

Tourmaline

Tourmaline – October Birthstone

Tourmaline is readily identified by its sequence of pink, green, yellow or blue colors. Often a crystal can have more than one color field in the same crystal. The color or depth changes if viewed from a different angle. Most tourmaline is strung in bands of alternating colors.

USA, Brazil, Italy, Sri Lanka, Pakistan, Russia

Rutilated Quartz

Tiger's Eye

Rutilated Quartz

Rutilated Quartz is clear quartz with golden or black needle-like inclusions of the mineral Rutile.

Rutile

Rutile is a metal which has industrial application because it is lightweight, strong and resistant to corrosion. Some crystals are thick with a black or reddish brown color or golden as thin crystals or inclusions in quartz. Also known as Venus hair or needle stone.

Australia, Brazil , Madagascar, South Africa Sri Lanka, USA

Chatoyant Quartz
Tiger's Eye

Tiger's Eye is brown/golden and contains golden fibrous inclusions of crocidolite that reflect light, creating a cat's-eye effect. This effect is called chatoyancy and is highlighted by the cut and polish.

Australia, Brazil, Burma, India, South Africa

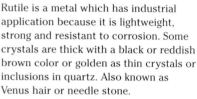

Garnet

Garnet – January Birthstone

Garnet is recognized by a deep reddish brown or wine color, which is commonly referred to as Almandine. It can also be a green color. This stone, called Tsavorite, comes from mines in Kenya.

Africa, India, Russia, Central America, South America.

Crazy Agate

Agate

Agate is called Banded Quartz. It is characterized by bands of exotic growth patterns displaying graduated values of a color or different colors. The name is derived from the river Achates in southwest Sicily. Agate varieties are identified by character and color.

Brazil, USA, Mexico and Germany

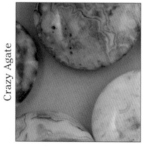

Moss Agate

Crazy Agate
Moss Agate
Blue Lace Agate

Blue Lace Agate

Blue Lace Agate is a pale periwinkle blue with faint white Agate-like markings. The stone takes a high polish and is frequently cut into lentils, or large facets, to highlight the delicate lacy patterns.

Eye Agate

Eye Agate – Sard, Sardonyx

Sard is similar to agate but has no banding, with reddish brown coloring. Sardonyx is a combination of sard and onyx. The bands in this type of agate are actually parallel instead of circular. The Egyptians carved scarabs, the English carved cameos and the Chinese often cut Sardonyx to reveal 'eyes'.

Malachite

Malachite

Malachite is an 'agate look alike', but not from the same family (it is a secondary copper mineral). Its name comes from the Greek word for "mallow", a green herb. It is banded with distinctive light and dark green designs, including radial clusters.

Congo, Namibia, Russia, Mexico, USA, Australia, England

Chalcedony

Chalcedony

Chalcedony is a minutely fine-grained (cryptocrystalline) variety of the silica mineral quartz. Its name originated from Chalcedon, an ancient port near Istanbul, Turkey. Chalcedony has a soft milky glow and is often dyed designer trend colors such as pink, blue or green. Varieties of Chalcedony include Agate, Carnelian, Chrysoprase, Moss Agate, Onyx and others.

Africa, Brazil, Uruguay

Jasper

Jasper is a colorful rock composed mostly of chalcedony, along with other minerals, which give it radical color bands and patterns. Jasper is often named according to its pattern or the location where it is found, such as ocean jasper mined off the coast of Madagascar. Other popular jaspers are: landscape jasper, Picasso jasper, needle jasper, ribbon jasper, picture jasper, and orbicular jasper.

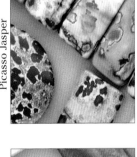

Picasso Jasper

Onyx – February Birthstone

Onyx is a rich black, nearly opaque gemstone. It is a variety of agate that has straight parallel bands, instead of curved bands. Pure black onyx is rare and commercial stones are often stained with a sugar-sulfuric acid treatment.

Carnelian

Carnelian is an abundant orange red stone ranging from milky to opaque. Carnelian gets its red tints from iron oxides. It is often carved into donuts, small figurines and charms.

Labradorite

Picture Jasper

Labradorite appears to be a dull, dark-looking mineral, but it is quickly transformed by an exquisite light shimmer seen glowing on the surface as it is viewed from various angles. The intense reflected colors range from blues and violets through greens, yellows and oranges. This is caused by rays of light bouncing back and forth within the stone, producing different wavelengths.

Ocean Jasper

Labradorite

The cut of the stone is crucial to highlight the beauty of Labradorite.

Labrador, Canada, Scandinavia

Oligoclase – June Birthstone

Oligoclase is best known as a semi-precious stone under the names of Sunstone and Moonstone. The glow of Moonstone is caused by rays of light reflecting back and forth within the stone. Moonstone often is strung in alternating colors of pale white, gray and pale reddish brown.

Sri Lanka, USA, Russia, Sweden, Canada.

Moonstone

Opal – October birthstone

Opal has the same chemical formula as quartz, but includes a small percentage of water trapped in tiny irregular spheres in the stone. This creates an effect of fire or flashes in the Opal. Peruvian Blue Opal is a delicate pale blue and often is cut with surrounding inclusions and host rock. Peruvian Pink Opal possesses a pale pink color. Translucency in the stone creates a dreamy velvet depth of color.

USA, Mexico, Australia, England, Czech Republic and several other places around the world.

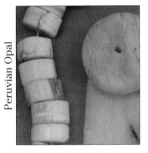

Peruvian Opal

Iolite

Iolite is the gem quality of the mineral Cordierite. The name iolite comes from the Greek word "ios", which means violet. Its color is a bluish purple to grayish black, with the most attractive stones being clear and well cut.

Sri Lanka, India Madagascar, Brazil, Burma, Zimbabwe

Lapis

Needle Jasper

Lapis lazuli or lapis is predominantly lazurite, but commonly contains pyrite, calcite and other minerals. The rich blue color is due to the sulfur contained in the structure of lazurite. The name means "blue rock" and was first mined 6000 years ago. It was once ground into the pigment ultramarine for oil paints. Lapis is a popular stone in the cultures of Tibet, India and Afghanistan, and the stone is often used in repoussee settings.

Afghanistan, Chile, Russia, Italy, USA

Sodalite

Onyx

Sodalite is a mineral named for its sodium content. It is essentially lapis, but lacks pyrite. It is used for carvings and some jewelry pieces. It is light to dark navy blue with white streaks (of calcite), gray, or even green.

Canada, Italy, Brazil, USA.

Peridot – August Birthstone

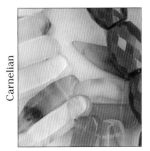

Carnelian

Peridot is the gem quality variety of mineral olivine, originally mined from the Topazos Island in the Egyptian Red Sea where use dates back several thousand years. It is a relatively clear stone with lime to olive color.

continued on pages 30 - 31

Rock & Stone Identification

You can't help but chuckle at some the fictitious nicknames given to polished stones. Is there really such a stone as Kiwi Quartz? Or Sesame Quartz?

I have seen the same stone with both names. I also smile at the reference to peanut jasper, zebra stone, and crazy agate, but can easily bring the image of the stones to mind.

Nicknames serve a purpose. Sometimes nicknames will denote a place of origin, as in 'Ocean Jasper' which is actually mined from the ocean shore of Africa.

One of my favorite names is Picasso Jasper dubbed after the bold and dynamic graphic veins and color contrasts in the stones.

Lapis

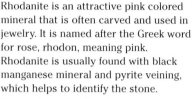

Sodalite

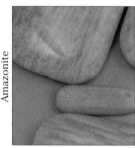

Rhodanite

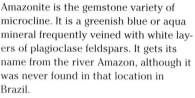

Amazonite

Aquamarine

continued from pages 28 - 29

USA, Burma, Pakistan

Rhodanite

Rhodanite is an attractive pink colored mineral that is often carved and used in jewelry. It is named after the Greek word for rose, rhodon, meaning pink. Rhodanite is usually found with black manganese mineral and pyrite veining, which helps to identify the stone.

Russia, Australia, Sweden, Brazil, USA

Rhodacrosite

Rhodacrosite is a pink stone with white bands often resembling agate.

Rhodalite

Rhodalite is a clear raspberry pinkish red crystal.

Amazonite

Amazonite is the gemstone variety of microcline. It is a greenish blue or aqua mineral frequently veined with white layers of plagioclase feldspars. It gets its name from the river Amazon, although it was never found in that location in Brazil.

Aquamarine – March Birthstone

Aquamarine is the blue-green or aqua variety of the mineral Beryl. It appears as a crystal or quartz-looking stone, sometimes with very pale color, mostly blue or blue-green. Aquamarine is colored by trace amounts of iron in the crystal structure and the deeper and clearer the color, the more valuable the stone. Emerald is the green variety of Beryl. It is exceptionally clear with deep coloring.

Brazil, USA, Russia, Africa.

Ruby – July Birthstone
Sapphire - September birthstone

Ruby is the red and Sapphires are the deep blue gemstone variety of the mineral corundum. The red color in ruby is caused by trace amounts of chromium in the stone. Ruby is commonly a deep blood red, but can be a pasty dark magenta or purple/red color. Small stones are often faceted in a variety of popular shapes and graduated sizes.

Thailand, India, Madagascar, Zimbabwe,

Ruby

Lemon Quartz

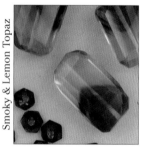

Smoky & Lemon Topaz

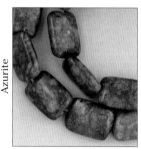

Azurite

Turquoise

USA, Afghanistan, Pakistan, Sri Lanka, Kenya, Tanzania, Kampuchea, Burma.

Topaz – November birthstone

Topaz is the hardest silicate mineral possessing high luster and appealing colors including pale tones of yellow, blue, green, pink and brown. Topaz can be heated or radiated resulting in different or deeper colors. Topaz is recognized by its clarity, and if the stone is not clear, it is more accurately identified as quartz.

Brazil, Russia, Australia, USA, Pakistan, Japan, Ireland Norway, Sweden, Nigeria, Germany, Sri Lanka, China

Azurite

Azurite derives its name from its azure blue color. The color results from the presence of copper and the way the copper chemically combines with other minerals. It often occurs with green Malachite that forms deposits on Azurite crystals and makes the soft stone more stable. Azurite has been ground and processed as a blue pigment for paints and fabrics.

Tsumeb, Namibia, USA, Australia

Turquoise – December Birthstone

Turquoise has an intense baby or robin egg blue color, although it can also be a greenish or brownish blue color, depending on the inclusions and place where it was mined. It is often mottled with veins of brown limonite or black manganese oxide. Color and purity and cut dictate the value of the stone. Use of turquoise dates back to the ancient Egyptians and is also recognized in adornments of the southwest Native American, Aztec, and Tibetan cultures. The name comes from a French word meaning stone of Turkey where the stones passed through on their way to Europe. Some Turquoise on the market is actually a white stone (usually Howlite) that has been dyed in an electroplating process. The price usually reflects the authenticity of the stone.

USA, England, Australia, Siberia, France, Germany, Chile, China.

Chrysoprase – May Birthstone

Chrysoprase is a delicate green between

Chrysoprase

Chrysocolla

Jade

Jade

Serpentine

Fluorite

lime and mint. The name comes from the Greek cryos meaning gold and prason meaning leek. The more predominant the color of green, the more valuable the stone.

Chrysocolla

Chrysocolla is an appealing stone with unique green-blue color similar to a copper patina. Chrysocolla originates in the oxidation zones of copper rich ore bodies, the reason for its captivating colors and inclusions of host ore. It is a fairly soft stone, and is usually cut in large chunks to accentuate the color.

USA, Scotland, Australia, France, Congo

Jade – Jadeite, Nephrite

Jadeite

Jadeite is one of the two minerals called jade. The other mineral is Nephrite, a variety of actinolite. Jade has been treasured for centuries in China and Central America as an ornamental and religious stone of deep significance. It is extremely hard and was utilized by many early civilizations for axes, knives and weapons. The most valuable jade is emerald green jade called "Imperial Jade", which is relatively rare. Jadeite jade also comes in lavender, pink, yellow and white. Nephrite jade displays less intense dark spinach greens, whites, browns and black. Many of the stones sold today as jade are not actually jade, but serpentine.

Australia, Burma, Canada, Taiwan, USA

Serpentine

Serpentine is a group of common minerals often rich in metal ores such as chromium, manganese, cobalt and nickel. Presence of these ores give the stone a variety of colors ranging from pale green to warm gold or dark brown. Most serpentines are opaque to transparent. Colors range from white to gray, yellow to green, and brown to black. The stone is predominantly popular in Asian cultures and is used to carve symbolic artifacts and adornments.

Canada, USA, Afghanistan, China, France, Norway, Italy, England, Russia

Fluorite

Fluorite is a relatively soft mineral, suitable for carving. It has a glassy luster and intense rich coloring of purple, yellow, pink, dark orange, blue, green, colorless, brown and black. The name comes from the Latin word Fluere, meaning to flow, derived from its use as flux in the smelting of iron.

Asia, England, Europe, USA,

Beryl

Beryl predominantly occurs as an inclusive mineral in granites. Pure Beryl is colorless, but impurities cause diverse colors. Emerald is the green variety and Aquamarine is the blue variety of Beryl.

Emerald – May Birthstone

The gemstone Emerald has a deep woodsy green possessing exceptional clarity. Its green color is caused by small amounts of chromium and iron in the beryl. Emerald has been historically cherished by the Egyptians, Hindus, Aztecs and Incas.

Afghanistan, Australia, Austria, Brazil, Columbia, India, Madagascar, Mozambique, Pakistan, Russia, South Africa, USA

Corundum

Corundum is the second hardest natural mineral known on earth (Diamond is 4 times harder). The color can be white, colorless, blue, red, yellow, green, pink, brown, and purple. Corundum is also known for the two more colorful varieties of gemstone, ruby and sapphire.

Burma, Sri Lanka, USA, Africa, India, Asia

Diamond – April Birthstone

Diamond is the most exquisite gemstone and is the hardest substance found in nature. It is the best conductor of heat and has the most refractive brilliance of any natural mineral. It possesses exceptional luster and has the ability to break up white light into a rainbow of color. Diamond colors include clear, yellow, brown, green, blue, pink, and rarely red.

Australia, Brazil, Russia, South Africa, USA

The one that didn't develop as planned.
All that shimmers is not attractive. This green Peridot beaded necklace just did not come together from my perspective.

Even though all the components are quality, it's really plain. Don't be discouraged because you have to disassemble and start again.

It's worth the experience to know the good pieces are exceptional and not everything always works out as you visualize.

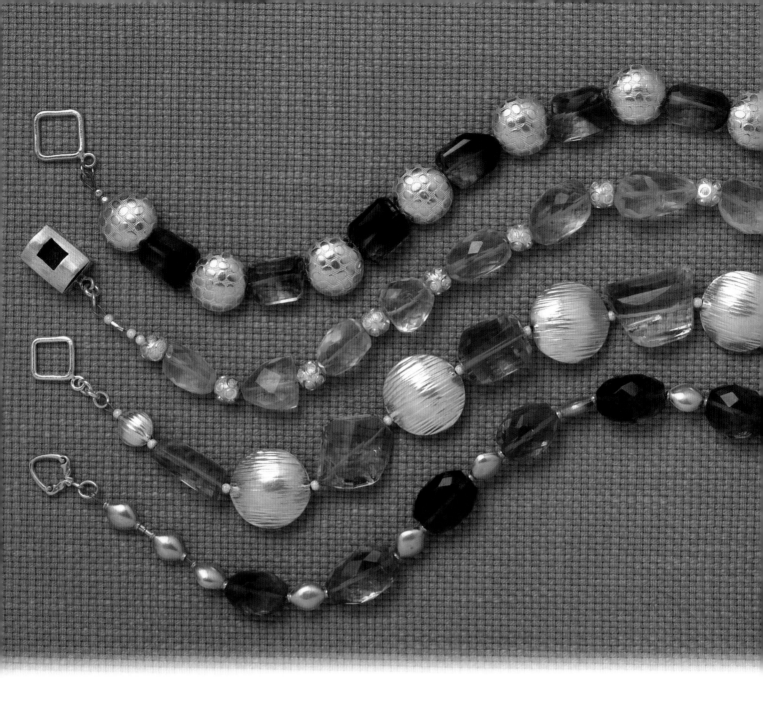

Necklaces (above)

Necklace 1: 15mm Lemon & Smoky Topaz Quartz stones • 12mm Gold beads • Basic supplies

Necklace 2: 15 - 25mm Lemon Quartz stones • 7mm Silver spacer beads • Basic supplies

Necklace 3: 20 - 25mm Citrine stones • 10mm Silver beads • 25mm Silver beads • 2mm Silver spacer beads • Basic supplies • Clasp by Jess Imports

Necklace 4: 20mm Amethyst stones • 12mm Gold spacer beads • Basic supplies

Stylish Set (page 33)

Necklace: 6mm Pearls • 5mm Green faceted beads • 1mm Gold spacer beads • Basic supplies

Bracelet: 6mm Pearls • 5mm Green faceted beads • 1mm Gold spacer beads • Basic supplies

Earrings: 6mm Freshwater Pearls • 2 mm faceted Peridot beads • 1mm Gold Vermeil spacer beads • Gold head pins • Gold earring wires

Stylish Sets

Expand your design theme to a complete set for a classic fashion statement. Shown, Peridot faceted gemstones, vermeil spacer beads and 6mm fresh water pearls.

What's Vermeil?

Vermeil is actually sterling silver that is gold plated, usually with 22K gold making the color deep and lasting.

Stunning Stones

The quality inherent in crystal stones is enhanced by the cut of the stone. Facets are no longer traditional and stones can be cut to enable the largest shape possible.

The quality of quartz, crystal and topaz is determined by the color and clarity of the stone. Quartz is rather milky and fractured and is often dyed as in cherry quartz.

Topaz possesses the highest clarity of the crystalline structures and is prized for its natural colors. In these necklaces, some traders would call the light yellow stone a lemon topaz, but it is not clear enough to warrant being a topaz and is more correctly identified as lemon quartz.

The first strand is dramatically clearer and identified as lemon and smoky topaz.

The next gem is citrine. Although these stones have brilliant clarity, there are still fissures that prevent them from being super high quality gems.

The last stones are amethyst crystals. Because of their clarity, they have a higher quality than milkier stones or quartz.

Strands of elegant stones are often too heavy or expensive to use abundantly in a necklace. Use fewer stones and enhance the design by choosing complementary beads that do not compete with the beautiful stones.

Dramatic Shapes

An artist usually gravitates to a preferential style or use of a learned skill in bead making with specialized materials... such as lampwork glass, resin, precious metal (Silver) clay or polymer clay.

The pieces here display artistic use of polymer clay, a modeling material that produces a wide range of effects including transfer images, canes, mokume gane surface design, and 'faux stone' with stamped impressions. In this case natural stones enhance the artistic focal bead.

Playful use of the differing shapes and forms creates a look that is striking, fresh and modern. As in stones, no two pieces are alike and each work is treasured for its unique quality.

Necklace 1: 38mm Polymer clay focal bead • 7mm Amazonite dagger stone beads • 20mm Chrysoprase beads • 3mm Gold beads • 1mm Gold spacer beads • Basic supplies

Necklace 2: 25 x 45mm Polymer clay focal bead • 4mm Shell dagger stone beads • 23mm Pink Jasper round beads • 20mm Thai Silver spiral beads • Silver spacer beads (2mm, 5mm) • Basic supplies

Necklace 3: 40 x 40mm Polymer clay focal bead • 25 x 35mm African Ocean Jasper beads • 9mm Gold Vermeil spacer beads • Basic supplies

MANY THANKS to my friends for their cheerful help and wonderful ideas!

Kathy McMillan • Shelley Riddell
Donna Kinsey • Diana McMillan • Janie Ray
David & Donna Thomason